Decipher The Word Of God

Decipher The Word Of God

OrangeBooks Publication

Smriti Nagar, Bhilai, Chhattisgarh - 490020

Website: **www.orangebooks.in**

First Edition, 2021

ISBN: 978-93-90837-39-7

Printed in India

DECIPHER THE WORD OF GOD

Dr. ATIF MURAD

OrangeBooks Publication

www.orangebooks.in

Dedicated to my son
Ali

جب غمسار ہے سراپا آلم ، ہے کوئی مسیحا درکار
شادابئ دل خدا حافظ کے علیار چلے ہے اُس پار

When the whole world is sad, a Messiah is awaited
Happiness of Heart, Goodbye, dear Ali has crossed
to other side

Acknowledgements

I would like to thank my beautiful wife, Nausheen for her feedback on the book but mostly for putting up with my odd working hours, while writing the book.

Thanks are due to my younger brother, Dr. Ameed Murad, and sister, Dr. Firdous Murad, being the first two, to go through the entire book and providing encouragement and suggestions.

I would like to include my daughter, Hanna, not for providing any feedback for the book, but for being my inspiration for doing anything, including living.

Also, my nephew, Yusuf and niece, Maryam for their love.

I am greatly indebted to my closest friends, Suhail A Siddiqui and Mobeen R Khan for providing valuable insight and encouraging me to proceed to publish this book.

The biggest contribution, however, is of my parents who introduced me to the Word of God, at an early age.

Contents

(Foreword

I like to start by saying that I am no scholar and I have received no structured religious instruction. All I present is logic hoping to appeal to a sound mind. The objective of this book is not that you should agree with what I say. Just hear me out and if you don't like what is presented, it's just an opinion and everyone is entitled to one.

Ever since I was in 7th grade I had a keen interest in books, novels mainly at that time. Over time, I got into serious reading. I was always intrigued by religion and philosophy. I read the scriptures that are easily available in English and the work of Philosophers and Scholars. I read from diverse sources and schools of thought.

Even for the religious books, I was not instructed by anyone. I looked up to two scholars of this time and wanted to benefit from them. I had access to them, at a personal level but got no further than just exchanging pleasantries. They both, left the World while I was still in Medical School. I did however read their works, and I consider whoever I read from as my teacher, although I may not be a worthy disciple.

What I present in the Book, if at places it is blunt and straight-forward, I don't mean to offend anybody, I was tempted to mellow down to be pleasing to everybody, but then I would have not done justice to the topic at hand. I would love to call all the ideas, presented in the book, mine, but I know that would not be correct. For I believe that even your thoughts, you can't claim to be your own. Plato in his works credited Socrates for all the ideas and did not claim them to be his own, although Socrates did not document them. Likewise, Divan-i Shams-i Tabrizi (The Works of Shams of Tabriz(RA)) was written by Rumi(RA).

All knowledge in the world, be it in any language or form, is coming from one true source who is, The Most Wise, The All Knowing, The Living, The Eternal, and the Only One Worthy of Worship.

The Code

The objective of this book is not to provide an explanation or commentary of the Holy Scriptures, but to develop your interest in the Word of God. So that you may read it with understanding and find yourself, the answers that you are looking for.

I refrain from providing my understanding unless utmost necessary to the topic. I wish to inspire you to read the scriptures on your own and not spoil your journey.

The Word

Here let me give you an interesting comparison between Jesus (peace be upon him) and Quran. Apart from the fact that they are both referred to as the Word of God, and brought to our World by the same Archangel, Gabriel(pbuh). Both were brought from the presence of the Lord without any human intervention, one to the Blessed Womb of Mary(pbuh) and the other to the Blessed Heart of

Prophet Mohammed(pbuh). Both are considered as miracles, a child born to a virgin, and a literary masterpiece from the blessed tongue of an unlettered Prophet(pbuh). They are both considered as Guides or Ways to God. There is debate regarding both of them, whether they are Divine or Creation of the Divine.

One of our Great Imam and scholar, Ahmad Bin Hanbal (RA) was severely beaten till he lost consciousness and jailed for over two years during the early reign of Caliph Al-Mutawakkil, because he did not accept that the Quran is created.

The One Who Converses With God

Moving on to the topic at hand, let me provide a few quotes-

Quran:Chapter (4) sūrat l-nisāa (The Women), verse 164

وَرُسُلًا قَدْ قَصَصْنَهُمْ عَلَيْكَ مِن قَبْلُ وَرُسُلًا لَّمْ نَقْصُصْهُمْ عَلَيْكَ وَكَلَّمَ ٱللَّهُ مُوسَىٰ تَكْلِيمًا ﴿١٦٤﴾

and to Musa (Moses) Allah spoke directly.

(Just took the translation of the 2nd part of the verse)

From the Bible,

"When there is a prophet among you,

I, the Lord, reveal myself to them in visions,

I speak to them in dreams.

But this is not true of my servant Moses;

he is faithful in all my house.

With him I speak face to face,

clearly and not in riddles;

Numbers 12, NIV

(please don't take the meaning of face to face, literally.)

God in his wisdom, talked to the Prophets in code, except for Moses(pbuh). For when the All-Mighty would speak to Moses(pbuh), it would be in plain language. That is the Station of Moses(pbuh) and He is aptly called Kaleem Ullah (the one who converses with God).

What No-One Knows

Let's examine the opening verse of the Quran. Some would say that it's Surah Fatiha while others think Surah Fatiha, is a summary of the Quran, given to you in the beginning. I prefer the latter view.

By opening verse, I mean-

Chapter (2) sūrat l-baqarah (The Cow)

Alif, Lam, Meem.

The very first verse of the Quran is just three alphabets, no one knows the meaning. So, we start with a code. If the Prophet(pbuh) told the meaning to some of the Sahabas (Companions), may God be pleased with them, they did not bring it out in the open. There are many instances like this one in the Quran. Apart from these types of verses, there are numerous verses which are translated differently by different Scholars and to many, no one knows the meaning or comes forward to offer one.

Men of Understanding

Let's consider the following verse. A lot of people refer to this verse to discourage you from looking for deeper meaning in the Quran.

Chapter (3) sūrat āl 'im'rān (The Family of Imrān), verse 7

هُوَ ٱلَّذِىٓ أَنزَلَ عَلَيْكَ ٱلْكِتَٰبَ مِنْهُ ءَايَٰتٌ مُّحْكَمَٰتٌ هُنَّ أُمُّ ٱلْكِتَٰبِ وَأُخَرُ مُتَشَٰبِهَٰتٌ ۖ فَأَمَّا ٱلَّذِينَ فِى قُلُوبِهِمْ زَيْغٌ فَيَتَّبِعُونَ مَا تَشَٰبَهَ مِنْهُ ٱبْتِغَآءَ ٱلْفِتْنَةِ وَٱبْتِغَآءَ تَأْوِيلِهِ ۗ وَمَا يَعْلَمُ تَأْوِيلَهُۥٓ إِلَّا ٱللَّهُ ۗ وَٱلرَّٰسِخُونَ فِى ٱلْعِلْمِ يَقُولُونَ ءَامَنَّا بِهِۦ كُلٌّ مِّنْ عِندِ رَبِّنَا ۗ وَمَا يَذَّكَّرُ إِلَّآ أُولُوا۟ ٱلْأَلْبَٰبِ ﴿٧﴾

He it is Who has sent down to thee the Book: In it are verses basic or fundamental (of established meaning); they are the foundation of the Book: others are allegorical. But those in whose hearts is perversity follow the part thereof that is allegorical, seeking discord, and searching for its hidden meanings, but no one knows its hidden meanings except Allah. And those who are firmly grounded in knowledge say: "We believe in the Book; the whole of it is from our Lord:" and none will grasp the Message except men of understanding.

Translated by Yusuf Ali

It is mentioned that no one knows the hidden meaning except Allah. So, it is established that there is a hidden meaning. Do you think Allah had put these verses with hidden meaning in the Quran for Himself? While we are his target audience. What would be the purpose of that? What is said here is that the people who have perversity in their hearts, obviously not worthy of divine knowledge, look for a deeper meaning to justify their twisted viewpoints and don't get to the true meaning. For only God knows the true meaning and Allah gives knowledge of the Quran to those whom he refers to as firmly grounded in knowledge and the men of understanding. There is no point in calling them firmly grounded in knowledge and the men of understanding if all they know is the basic, straightforward, and the fundamental. How will they be different from you and me?

Let's consider the case of an old person in possession of a treasure, who has young children. The old man hides the treasure and writes down the directions to get to the treasure. To make sure that the treasure doesn't get into the wrong hands, he codes the directions and only teaches his sons how to decode the way to the treasure.

Let's look at the following verse.

Chapter (73) sūrah muzamil (The One wrapped in Garments), verse 6

إِنَّ نَاشِئَةَ ٱلَّيْلِ هِىَ أَشَدُّ وَطْـًٔا وَأَقْوَمُ قِيلًا ﴿٦﴾

Verily, the rising by night (for Tahajjud prayer) is very hard and most potent and good for governing (the soul), and most suitable for (understanding) the Word (of Allah).

If all that you should study is fundamental, why do you need to get up at night to understand the Word? The nighttime is mentioned here because at that time, it's calm and quiet and you are not occupied. Also, there is no one to disturb you, so you can concentrate.

Let me present to you a few examples from Quran and Hadith.

Example of symbology of Stars and Trees

A lot of verses are like dreams, you don't take them literally, they need to be interpreted.

Chapter (12) sūrat yūsuf (Joseph)

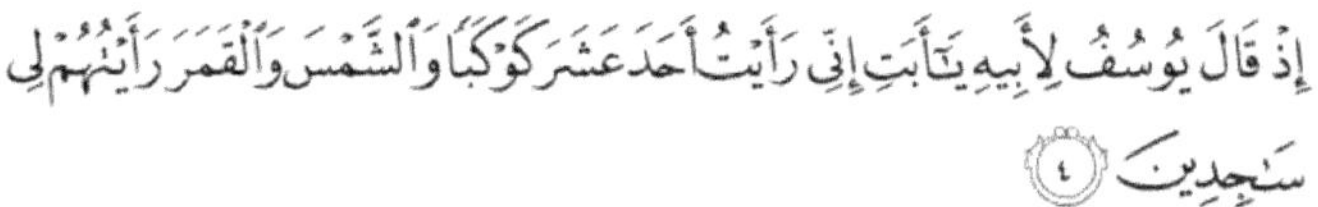

(Remember) when Yusuf (Joseph) said to his father: "O my father! Verily, I saw (in a dream) eleven stars and the sun and the moon, I saw them prostrating themselves to me."

Here I will only pick out the stars and what they represent for a later discussion. In this case, the stars, as you probably already know, represent the brothers of Joseph. They were forgiven, by Joseph and God elevated them to be Prophets for their tribes. A star usually symbolizes a Guide.

Now let's look at a Hadith.

Narrated Ibn 'Umar:

Allah's Apostle said, "Amongst the trees, there is a tree, the leaves of which do not fall and is like a Muslim. Tell me the name of that tree." Everybody started thinking about the trees of the desert areas. And I thought of the date-palm tree but felt shy to answer, the others then asked, "What is that tree, O

Allah's Apostle?" He replied, "It is the date-palm tree." Sahih Bukhara Volume 1, Book 3, Number 58

Here we learn that the date-palm tree represents a Muslim. The only characteristic mentioned here of the tree is that its leaves do not fall. I would want to know, what that symbolizes? I doubt you will get any satisfactory answer.

Anyway, let's move on to a verse in the Quran.

Chapter (55) sūrat l-raḥmān (The Most Gracious), verse 6

$$وَٱلنَّجْمُ وَٱلشَّجَرُ يَسْجُدَانِ ﴿٦﴾$$

And the stars and trees prostrate.

Does this combination of stars and trees, surprise you? Why would the All-Wise talk about the stars and trees together? And telling us, that they prostrate, while we have no idea how they are linked? and how they prostrate? Let me remind you, we are the target audience of God.

Now let's replace the star with Guide or Prophet from the previous example and get the tree to represent a man or a Muslim from the Hadith. Now the Verse could be interpreted as Prophets and Muslims Prostrating.

This is just a demonstration you don't have to agree with me. In my support, I will give another verse.

Chapter (12) sūrat yūsuf (Joseph), verse 7

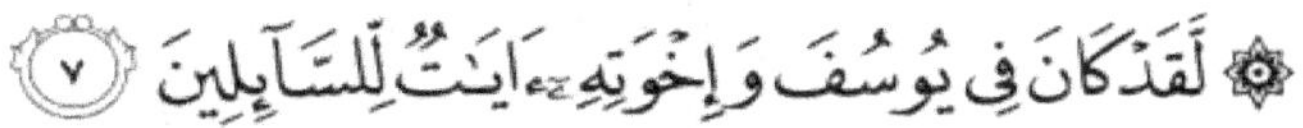

Verily in Joseph and his brethren are signs (or symbols) for seekers (after Truth).

Yusuf Ali

Example of Symbology of House, Dog and Picture

Narrated Abu Talha:

The Prophet (ﷺ) said, "Angels do not enter a house that has either a dog or a picture in it."

Sahih al-Bukhari 3322

I am sure you have heard of this Hadith and banished dogs from your house and removed pictures and portraits from the walls.

Before, I put forward my understanding of the Hadith. I ask, what is the purpose of all Hadith? For that, let me quote two Hadith-

The Prophet Muhammad(pbuh) said "I was sent to perfect good character."

Malik, Book 47, Hadith 1643

And

The Prophet (pbuh)said 'The best among you are those who have the best manners and character '

(Bukhari, Vol 008, Book 073, Hadith Number 056B)

In Ihya Ulum-din, According to Imam Ghazali (RA), the four attributes found in the heart are lust, anger, divine, and satanic inclinations. And in Kimya-Saadet we find-

The faculty of reason may be likened to a hunter on horseback. The power of lust is like the horse, and the power of anger is like his dog. In this regard, whenever the horseman is a master and both his horse and dog well-trained, the circumstances are appropriate for the horseman to be victorious.

Now in light of the Hadith and the sayings of Imam Ghazali (RA), The House is your Heart, the Dog represents Anger, the pictures or image is the idol you revere. That idol could be your guide, whom you elevate in your love and respect, even unconsciously, to be a rival to God.

Angles don't have anything against the dogs, they are just like other animals. The Ashab e Kahf (sleepers or the companions of the cave) spoken of so highly by the All-Merciful in the Quran had a dog with them.

Let me quote from the Gospel. Jesus(pbuh) said -

Do not give dogs what is holy; do not throw your pearls before swine. If you do, they may trample them under their feet, and then turn and tear you to pieces.

Matthew 7:6 BSB

Here the pearls represent sacred knowledge, dogs and swine represent unworthy men and not the actual animals. If unworthy men are informed of some divine secret which they are unable to digest, They become angry (the dog) and attack the Holy Person.

An angry person is said to have the dog in the heart, because of his behavior. He is barking at you, is ready to bite and attack you. Don't take anger lightly, it's one of the major vices of the spiritual heart, some other being stinginess, pride, envy, hypocrisy, lust, and greed.

Coming back to the Hadith, now it means that the angles visit the heart as long as you have character and refrain from ascribing partners to the One Worthy of Worship.

Learning To Decipher

You must be wondering, why all the symbolism in the previous two examples. The meaning after interpretation is also straightforward and there is no hidden meaning. Why isn't what is meant to be said, said in plain language.

Well, examples like these are just to get you going, once you solve these and get the hang of decoding, you move on to tougher verses of the Quran and Hadith, which will have a deeper meaning. A lot of it is just cross-referencing different portions of the Quran and Hadith. What is mentioned in one place is explained in another place. It's a difficult task because of the sheer volume of the Quran and Hadith. A good memory is very helpful. Now, if God is smiling at you, he will lead you to deeper meanings.

If you do get to deeper meaning, do not boast or broadcast it to anyone and keep the verse that I mentioned in your mind. God only knows if you got to the true meaning and you may not be correct in your understanding. If you do get to the true meaning, you will be silent, for it is nourishment for your journey and you are still some distance away from your destination.

Also, if you share your understanding with others, the meaning might hurt them and they, in turn, might hurt you.

Example of a Verse left Unexplained

Chapter (19) sūrat maryam (Mary), verse 28

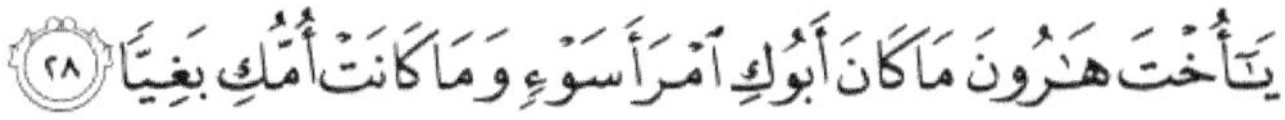

O sister of Aaron, your father was not a man of evil, nor was your mother unchaste."

Sahih International

There is a lot of controversy regarding what is said above. If you are not aware, please look it up. I will not be going into the history of it. I will quote first what the critics of Islam have to say. You will find a list at the mentioned URL in the reference section. I am just quoting one of them.

From Islamic Awareness website-

Alphonse Mingana reiterated the same claim:

Who then will not be astonished to learn that in the Qur'ân, Miriam, the sister of Aaron, is confounded with the Virgin Mary?

A hadith-

Mughira ibn Shu'ba reported: When I came to Najran, the Christian monks asked me, "You recite the verse: O sister of Aaron (19:28), whereas Moses was born long before Jesus by such-and-such years." When I came back to the Messenger of Allah, peace and blessings be upon him, I asked him about it and he said:

Verily, they would name people with the names of prophets and righteous people who had gone before them.

Sahih Muslim 2135

The critics to this day are not satisfied with the answer provided in this Hadith. I didn't include the response of Muslim Scholars, as they have not been able to give a reasonable answer acceptable to the critics, according to whom, this is the weakest link in the Quran.

The Prophet(pbuh) had already answered, and the people of the Book, who knew the scriptures, probably understood the answer. They would have expected no more, from a true Prophet, than what was said.

I am sure you must be getting uneasy and wondering why I brought this verse.

Let's draw your attention to How God inspired the Prophet(pbuh) to respond to the questions that were put to him by some of the Children of Israel.

Chapter (17) sūrat l-isrā (The Night Journey), verse 85

وَيَسْـَٔلُونَكَ عَنِ ٱلرُّوحِ قُلِ ٱلرُّوحُ مِنْ أَمْرِ رَبِّى وَمَآ أُوتِيتُم مِّنَ ٱلْعِلْمِ إِلَّا قَلِيلًا ﴿٨٥﴾

And they ask you (O Muhammad SAW) concerning the Ruh (the Spirit); Say: "The Ruh (the Spirit): it is one of the things, the knowledge of which is only with my Lord. And of knowledge, you (mankind) have been given only a little."

Here I am surprised by the courage shown by those who asked about the Ruh (Spirit). They wanted no less than the mother of Pearls from the Prophet(pbuh), without diving themselves in the Ocean. The answer of Prophet(pbuh) told them nothing about the Ruh. Likewise coming back to the supposed weakest link, God in his wisdom withheld the knowledge of that verse from becoming common and inspired what the Prophet said. Now when the Prophet did not elaborate do you think the people to whom the knowledge was passed on by the Prophet would dare to explain, no matter how much embarrassment they have to go through.

God Under No Obligation

People are hasty. Critics object to the above-mentioned verse and the other objection is regarding the period of Hamaan. I am not going into details of Hamaan, it's the same question. Please research if you are interested. These are two instances out of over 6000 verses of the Quran. If they don't understand the meaning of the verses, perhaps they are lacking in the knowledge of their scriptures.

God, or His Prophets(pbuh), are under no obligation to provide answers or spoon feed knowledge to anybody. God does what He wills and guides whom He wills.

Do you think, that our father, Adam(pbuh) did something to deserve the knowledge and station he received, to which even the Angles objected. It was a gift, and when God asked Adam(pbuh) to display his knowledge, the Angles realized their mistake.

Chapter (2) sūrat -baqarah (The Cow), verse 3

قَالُوا سُبْحَانَكَ لَا عِلْمَ لَنَا إِلَّا مَا عَلَّمْتَنَا إِنَّكَ أَنتَ الْعَلِيمُ الْحَكِيمُ ﴿٣٢﴾

They (angels) said: "Glory be to You, we have no knowledge except what you have taught us. Verily, it is You, the All-Knower, the All-Wise."

Quran & Bible

The Quran is full of Biblical references and the biographies of the Prophets mentioned in the Bible. Let me clarify, Quran is talking about the same topic but the information provided is not the same, mostly. Rather Quran defends the Prophets who were wrongly maligned in the Old Testament, by showing them to be men of high character and as ideals to look up to. Quoting just the defence of Solomon(pbuh) below.

And they followed [instead] what the devils had recited during the reign of Solomon. It was not Solomon who disbelieved, but the devils disbelieved, teaching people magic.

Surah Baqarah, verse 102

The Quran descended in over 23 years. During that time, God challenged the critics of that time to produce the likeness of the Quran.

Chapter (10) sūrat yūnus (Jonah), verse 38

$$ أَمْ يَقُولُونَ ٱفْتَرَىٰهُ ۖ قُلْ فَأْتُوا۟ بِسُورَةٍ مِّثْلِهِۦ وَٱدْعُوا۟ مَنِ ٱسْتَطَعْتُم مِّن دُونِ ٱللَّهِ إِن كُنتُمْ صَٰدِقِينَ ﴿٣٨﴾ $$

Or do they say [about the Prophet], "He invented it?" Say, "Then bring forth a surah like it and call upon [for assistance] whomever you can besides Allah, if you should be truthful."

The Origin of Mankind

The narration of Adam(pbuh), Eve, and Satan is spread out in the Quran at numerous places. Every time the narration comes, you get some new information. God did not just put it in one place. You got to fit the pieces together and look at the complete picture. What happened in the Garden of Eden has puzzled Jewish, Christian, and Muslim scholars alike.

The Guide

Let me begin this chapter with the first five verses of the Quran in in the name of God, the Most Merciful and the Most Compassionate.

Chapter (2) sūrat l-baqarah (The Cow)

Alif, Lam, Meem.

ذَٰلِكَ ٱلْكِتَٰبُ لَا رَيْبَ ۛ فِيهِ ۛ هُدًى لِّلْمُتَّقِينَ ﴿٢﴾

This is the Book about which there is no doubt, a guidance for those conscious of Allah –

ٱلَّذِينَ يُؤْمِنُونَ بِٱلْغَيْبِ وَيُقِيمُونَ ٱلصَّلَوٰةَ وَمِمَّا رَزَقْنَٰهُمْ يُنفِقُونَ ﴿٣﴾

Who believe in the unseen, establish prayer, and spend out of what We have provided for them,

وَٱلَّذِينَ يُؤْمِنُونَ بِمَا أُنزِلَ إِلَيْكَ وَمَا أُنزِلَ مِن قَبْلِكَ وَبِٱلْآخِرَةِ هُمْ يُوقِنُونَ ٤

And who believe in what has been revealed to you, [O Muhammad], and what was revealed before you, and of the Hereafter they are certain [in faith].

أُوْلَـٰٓئِكَ عَلَىٰ هُدًى مِّن رَّبِّهِمْ وَأُوْلَـٰٓئِكَ هُمُ ٱلْمُفْلِحُونَ ٥

Those are upon [right] guidance from their Lord, and it is those who are the successful.

Conditions of the Guide

Please forgive me, for being blunt right in the beginning and saying, you will not truly benefit from the Quran unless you are sincere in your pursuit of the truth. The word of the All-Mighty is not for casual reading. To show your sincerity, you must fulfill the conditions in Verse 3 and 4 above, then Verse 5 will apply to you.

Brothers don't be discouraged, if you can't fulfill these conditions right now. Approach the Quran, look at it carefully, take your time. if you are sincerely seeking the truth it will appeal to you and then you will be willing to comply with the conditions and benefit from the Guide.

Definition of Guide

Now let's analyze, what or who is a Guide? Well, a Guide is understood to be a person or a book as in this matter, that correctly shows you the way or makes you understand a matter which was vague to you previously.

If there is a guide available, would you rather go to the person standing next to him, or to a person who knows the guide, or is his brother or friend, instead of going directly to the guide?

Or would you rather take another less experienced guide to go to this guide? What if this worldly guide of yours takes forever for guiding you and this life is not enough. What if you are stuck with basic and mediocre stuff and miss out on the butter and honey.

So, I would not recommend that you take the easy way and start approaching the Quran through some explanation(tafseer) provided by a Scholar, for then you are learning Islam as understood by that scholar. Thinking what they are thinking or thought and following what they are doing or did.

Everybody is Unique

An old saying, ways to God are as diverse as the souls of men. Likewise, there are many tracks, leading to the top of the mountain. The track taken by somebody else might not be suitable for you, as you may have a different set of knowledge, skills, and experiences of life. You were made unique by the All-Mighty, given a unique fingerprint, DNA and Soul. Your life experiences are unique to you, you see the world through your unique eyes and have a different perspective of the world around you. Why shouldn't your way to your Creator be unique too? The real guides are those who will refrain from putting their explanation of verses to you, but rather have you ponder on the Quran and Sunnah and come up with your answers. The answers are there, and to the questions you have.

Approach The Quran

The sunnah or the way of the Prophet is the only other source you can trust. While the Prophet was with us, we did not need the Quran separately, as the Quran was contained inside his Heart. It's only after he has left us that we need the Quran as a Guide. The sunnah sheds light on the Quran and provides you with the code of conduct.

Someone would say, I don't know Arabic, what can I do if not read the explanation?

I would suggest learning Arabic, just the basic or intermediate would be enough to get you going, and you build on it. If learning Arabic is not an option, then I would suggest you read the translation of the Quran. Let me remind you, you are already at a handicap if you don't learn Arabic. But I am not going to discourage you from approaching the Quran, for God guides whom he wills.

Don't rush into the Quran, read a few verses or a page or two, but read every day, and ponder over its meaning. Don't plan on finish reading the Quran in a week or a month but take a year. Don't be sad when you reach the ending Chapter of the Quran, for there is not more to read of the Divine Word and you want more, just read again and it will be a whole new Quran. Every time you read the Quran, you build on your previous knowledge, and there is an unlimited supply.

Now you can benefit from the explanation (tafseer) of the scholars after you have grounded yourself in Quran and Hadith. The benefit is there in these worldly guides. If they are real, they can cultivate and boost your love for God. They can stir up your soul so that you have a longing for your Creator and a nostalgia for your real home. But that's all they can offer. They cannot hold your hand and lead you to the top of the mountain, for they are walking on their path. If you hold on to them you will be getting closer to them and not your destination. They will ignite the spark. You have to keep the fire burning so that you can walk in the darkness.

The Pearls

If you go to a guide these days, you should be sure that he has seen the view from the top of the mountain and came back to inspire others. The True guide will hide, for he has the pearls of wisdom, which he collected by diving deep into the ocean of knowledge of God. They are his life's earnings and will not give them to you or show them to you, for he fears that such an act might cause the pearls to lose their shine, or he would risk losing them, or he will not be getting any more pearls no matter how deep he dives. The pearls are not meant for everyone.

Jesus said in the gospel.

Do not give dogs what is holy; do not throw your pearls before swine. If you do, they may trample them under their feet, and then turn and tear you to pieces.

Matthew 7:6 BSB

If you are a deserving candidate and get close to one of these Guides, they might, out of love of God, throw a pearl or two in your direction.

I would still say, go to the source of pearls from where the guides picked up the pearls, The ocean of Knowledge, and dive yourself and look for pearls, for there is an abundant supply of them, and you get better at every dive.

So refrain from filling up your mind with the ideas and thoughts of others. Rather be a clean slate and ponder on the meaning of the verses of the Quran. Have custodian Angles of the Quran write on your soul and chart your intergalactic journey.

The Highway

All of us are on the journey, traveling with the speed of light. We are all on the Highway, and there are signs for the lanes and exits. The Angles are managing the traffic. Some people are changing lanes, others just following the traffic ahead, ignorant of the Signs on the Highway. The last exit on the Highway is for Hell and Heaven. Hell is on the left hand of the Highway and Heaven on the right. As the exit nears, the people are not allowed to change the lanes anymore. They are forced by the Angles to keep in their lanes. The majority of the lanes are turning towards Hell, few to Heaven and a single road continues straight ahead.

The Journey

Now, who needs a guide? Not the person who stays at home all the time. Even a blind person can easily find his, or her way at home. It's a person who takes on a journey, and that too in uncharted territory that needs a guide.

You would say the person staying at home, is not harming anybody and thus not sinning. Well, we are all supposed to take the journey, for our souls are yearning for the Creator. And to deny that journey to the soul is a great sin.

All those who spend their whole life just involved with the day-to-day life of this world (our stay-at-home guy), just wasted their precious life in mundane affairs. You should at least get the transistor out and send signals to see if someone is listening and if you hear back, you have made contact. You can start your journey. Someone who spends his whole life without making any type of contact with the Divine is going back in a loss.

Surah Asr In Quran-

1. By time,

إِنَّ ٱلْإِنسَٰنَ لَفِى خُسْرٍ ﴿٢﴾

2. Indeed, mankind is in loss,

إِلَّا ٱلَّذِينَ ءَامَنُوا۟ وَعَمِلُوا۟ ٱلصَّٰلِحَٰتِ وَتَوَاصَوْا۟ بِٱلْحَقِّ وَتَوَاصَوْا۟ بِٱلصَّبْرِ ﴿٣﴾

3. Except for those who have believed and done righteous deeds and advised each other to truth and advised each other to patience.

Some brothers don't believe that there is a journey. Let me remind them that they are instructed to call upon Allah, five times a day, asking for the straight path. (Siratal- Mustaqeem). They would say that's symbolic. So is the journey.

If there is no journey, why would you have a destination? Let me give you different translations of the ending of Verse (2:285) - The objective of iteration is to get the message across.

Sahih International:

[We seek] Your forgiveness, our Lord, and to You is the [final] destination."

Pickthall:

(Grant us) Thy forgiveness, our Lord. Unto Thee is the journeying.

Yusuf Ali:

(We seek) Thy forgiveness, our Lord, and to Thee is the end of all journeys."

Shakir:

Thy forgiveness (do we crave), and to Thee is the eventual course.

Muhammad Sarwar:

Lord, we need Your forgiveness and to You we shall return."

Mohsin Khan:

(We seek) Your Forgiveness, our Lord, and to You is the return (of all)."

Arberry:

Our Lord, grant us Thy forgiveness; unto Thee is the homecoming.'

You will find other similar verses in the Quran. I will not quote more. Please note, it is to God that is the homecoming and not to Paradise. Many would argue that it is Judgement Day, which is, referred to here. Well, Judgement Day is just a passing event, no matter how long it would be. How could a day be a destination? Paradise and Hell could classify as destinations.

It is not just a journey, it is a return journey, and the Quran is the reminder of it. No wonder Quran is also called Al-Dhikr by Allah, meaning The Remembrance or The Reminder. The Quran is not reminding you of Paradise, but of Allah. Paradise happens to be on the way.

The Spaceship

Don't be walking on the edges of the Ocean and that too holding somebody's hand. Drop everything and jump into the Ocean. Or rather, be in a one-man spaceship. The Quran as your navigation system, and your love of the Most-Merciful, being your fuel. Let there be an infinite amount of that fuel, and God Willing, you will get to your destination. I would say, if there is not enough fuel in your ship, and you start the journey, The Sustainer (Rab) will keep adding fuel or keep coming closer to you. For he says-

Whoever comes to Me walking, I will come to him running.

Ṣaḥīḥ Muslim 2687

The Sandals

Now, what do I mean by "drop everything", the same thing that Moses(pbuh) was asked to do when he approached the Burning Bush.

Chapter (20) sūrat ṭā hā, verse 12

إِنِّىٓ أَنَا۠ رَبُّكَ فَٱخْلَعْ نَعْلَيْكَ إِنَّكَ بِٱلْوَادِ ٱلْمُقَدَّسِ طُوًى ﴿١٢﴾

Indeed, I am your Lord, so remove your sandals. Indeed, you are in the sacred valley of Tuwa.

Sahih International Translation

The two sandals, according to Sheikh Abdul Qadir Jilani (RA) represent both the worlds.

Chapter (8) sūrat l-anfāl (The Spoils of War), verse 28

وَٱعْلَمُوٓاْ أَنَّمَآ أَمْوَٰلُكُمْ وَأَوْلَٰدُكُمْ فِتْنَةٌ وَأَنَّ ٱللَّهَ عِندَهُۥٓ أَجْرٌ عَظِيمٌ ﴿٢٨﴾

And know that your properties and your children are but a trial and that Allah has with Him a great reward.

Chapter (2) sūrat l-baqarah (The Cow)

وَمِنْهُم مَّن يَقُولُ رَبَّنَآ ءَاتِنَا فِى ٱلدُّنْيَا حَسَنَةً وَفِى ٱلْأَخِرَةِ حَسَنَةً وَقِنَا عَذَابَ ٱلنَّارِ ﴿٢٠١﴾

But among them is he who says, "Our Lord, give us in this world [that which is] good and in the

Hereafter [that which is] good and protect us from the punishment of the Fire."

Sahih International

A lot go people refer to the above verse to say there is nothing wrong with seeking the good things in this world. Please consider the verse above that. When your property and children do not classify as Hasana (good), what would? I am not implying that you should not love your children. Just that your love for God and the Prophet(pbuh) should be more. Sometimes the love of children and property are hindrances to your progress, and do not let you fly higher. According to Imam Ghazali (RA), Hasana (good) in the world are only devotion and knowledge.

Nothing drastic needs to be done. You just need to lessen your indulgence in the world at least for the time of the journey. What else, well the other sandal, which is the afterworld, you got to get rid of the desire of paradise as well. Sheikh Abdul Qadir Jilani (RA) says that the world is a veil for Paradise, and Paradise is a veil for God and that the true seeker of God would stand aside when asked to enter Paradise. He would say to the All-Mighty, I left the world for you and I would leave paradise as well for a glimpse of You. Because he knows that, there is nothing as Beautiful as God himself.

The Battleground

If you do your deeds in this world for the sake of getting into Paradise, then that's what you will get, if your deeds are accepted. You will not get, near to God for you did not do the deeds, to gain his pleasure or nearness. If you are confused already and would rather prefer your journey to Paradise, further reading would only bring more remorse.

For suffering is the way, the more you suffer the higher you rise. Among the people, it is the Prophets who suffered the most. Were they not dear to God? Were they not the Chosen Ones? This world is a battleground, you lose loved ones, get hurt, fall sick, lose money and property. Why all this suffering? Well, you are being tested, that is all this world is about. It's not real life. This is the testing ground for you, so you may collect points, deeds, for your afterlife, which is the true life. The life without death and suffering. The life with all the pleasures that you can imagine and beyond.

Adam to Muhammed

(Peace Be Upon Them)

The first journey was made by Adam(pbuh), with infinite love, our father made the journey back home easily, after all, he was taught by the Master himself. After his successful journey, he guided many among his progeny.

After Adam(pbuh), other Prophets came, and as long as there was one, he was the guide and the way. It's only when you don't have a prophet to guide you, you need a Guidance system.

A major development came with Moses(pbuh), when God decided to give properly documented guidance. So, the Torah provided Laws and Commandments for guidance and also cultivated the love for the Most-Holy. Supported later, by the Psalms of David(pbuh). Many people took the journey. But over time people did not either follow the Torah or lacked in their love for God, so God sent a series of prophets for their guidance. Although, they already had the book of Moses(pbuh). Then over time, the Holy Scriptures were tampered with for worldly gains.

Then came Jesus(pbuh), to fulfill the promises of the Old Testament and renewed the faith and the love of The Father in Heaven through the Gospel.

Jesus(pbuh) upheld the Commandments of Moses(pbuh). He performed all sorts of miracles, including walking on water and healing the lepers. He showed mercy to the sinners and a multitude of people made the journey.

Then Jesus(pbuh) was taken up to heaven and the people were left with the old Guidance system and the Gospel. Now although people had a lot of love for the Creator, because of the teaching of Jesus(pbuh), they had no Guide. Then followers of Jesus(pbuh) did away with the laws and commandments provided by Moses(pbuh), altogether, contrary to the teaching of Jesus(pbuh).

"Do not think that I have come to abolish the Law or the Prophets; I have not come to abolish them but to fulfil them."

Matthew 5:17 NIV

As the people could no longer make the journey so God came to those who were bursting with love that Jesus(pbuh) had provided, to guide these people Himself. That's an exception. For when God comes to you, you don't need to take the journey, you have instant success. However, the vast majority of the people even if they had some love and faith, were directionless without any Guidance. The word for them in the Quran is Dualleen (the ones who went astray).

Now the dark ages start, a long time passes and no Prophet arrives, people are either waiting for the second coming of Jesus(pbuh) or the other Prophets of the Old Testament, namely Elijah(pbuh). Previously there was a chain and succession of Prophets from the time of Adam(pbuh). Sometimes there would be multiple Prophets present at the same time. But now, six hundred years had passed since Jesus(pbuh) left, and no True Guide had come.

To end these dark ages of ignorance comes the final Messenger of God, Muhammed(pbuh) with updated Guidance. The Quran kept most of the commandments of Moses(pbuh) and added a few. A multitude made the journey. Now as Prophet Muhammed (pbuh) was to be the last Messenger, there would be no Prophets following him, except of course for the second coming of Jesus(pbuh), which Prophet Muhammed(pbuh) himself foretold. But that is an exception. So, God had to make sure, that Prophet Muhammed(pbuh) left behind a Guidance for the ages to come. Now as this system had to last till the end of days, God provided a Firewall.

Chapter (15) sūrat l-ḥij'r (The Rocky Tract)

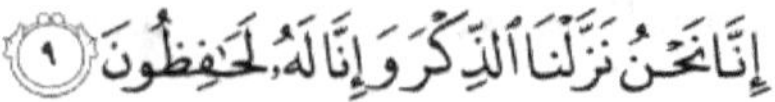

It is We Who have sent down the Dhikr (i.e. the Quran) and surely, We will guard it (from corruption).

Our Sorry State

Now again, very few people are taking the journey, although the guidance is intact. Few people seek it, for they do not have time even for themselves. They spend most of their lifetime working 9 to 5 with little time to offer for the family. They don't have a moment to zoom out and see the bigger picture. They don't realize what they are doing with their precious time? While the clock is ticking. The majority of the people have taken up loans for different reasons. They are now working for the Banks.

Others who may have some money, and are successful in worldly affairs, set up higher living standards. Then work to achieve them, are never content, and keep on setting higher standards. Yet others may be rich. They spend their life multiplying what they have and safeguarding it. They are in a race with each other to hoard more and more until the time on earth runs out.

Quran: Surah Takasur

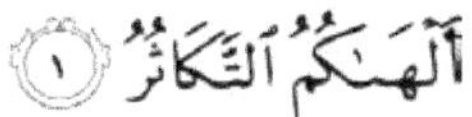

1. Competition in [worldly] increase diverts you

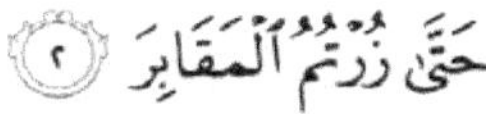

2. Until you visit the graveyards.

Some have their interpretations and notions about the Quran and stick blindly to them. For them the Quran, explained by a scholar revered by them is absolute, and would never look up the Quran itself. Mind you, these interpretations are not guaranteed to be free of error as they are produced by humans, in contrast to the Word of God, which is free of all errors.

"If [Quran] had been from other than Allah, they would have found within it much contradiction"

Sura 4:82

Or worse still they read the Quran and not understand a bit of what they read. They would read it fast and complete the whole Quran in a very short period, and then do it again and again, without understanding a single word. For the majority of Muslims in the world know how to read Arabic but they don't understand it.

As for the Love of the Most-Holy, we are in a pathetic state of materialism and worldly ambitions and character is missing. We are a sinful and ungrateful generation, destroying the nature around us and mankind alike. There is scarcity of Godly people and Evil reigns high. For God has taken away his favourite among mankind and taken away his knowledge with them. So, there are only a few if any left who can help people cultivate the love of the Creator.

Allama Iqbal says thus in his Jawab e Shikwa.

Tum Mein Hooron Ka Koi Chahne Wala Hi Nahin

Jalwa-e-Toor Tau Maujood Hai, Moosa Hi Nahin

Not a single one among you is longing for houris

The Effulgence of 'Tur' exists but there is no Moses

Well not even the graphic depictions of Paradise and Hours in the Quran is appealing to anyone, nor the deterrence of Hell, which are easier to cultivate in the common man than the true love of God.

Something grand needs to be done, and our leaders and scholars have failed for centuries now to provide the stimulus to improve the decaying condition of the people at large.

The Bridegroom

Our only hope is in Jesus(pbuh) now and God only knows what Jesus(pbuh) would do when he comes, as we are in the same sorry state as the people he was sent to before.

Jesus(pbuh) was sent down with Authority, and when he would be present, he will be the Guide, he will be the way.

Those who are waiting, get your ships ready before the Messiah comes, for you will take off with his single glance. Don't be like the virgins who fell asleep waiting for the bridegroom and their lamps ran out of oil. (Matthew 25)

The Child

You don't need to go anywhere such as a cave, the jungle, the top of the mountains or space for that matter. For the journey is within. It's just a change for a better You. You just need periods of solitude for some time and the night time is the best for that. Also, you need detachment from the world. You live in this world like before, performing your duties to the family and work, but the world no longer lives in you. For as long as the boat is above the water, it floats and the moment water gets into the boat it drowns.

So how long is the journey? It's different for everybody. Some may reach their destination in just one night and others may spend a lifetime. It all depends on how well you understand the Quran and apply it to you but largely it depends on what is bestowed upon you for your efforts. You do all the effort with all heart and mind and then wait for the results. I do say you have to make the effort, but the result or whatever is bestowed upon you is not due to your effort or deeds. It's all by the Grace of God. For your good deeds are also bestowed upon you as favour from God. So don't be proud of your deeds or expect anything in return.

Chapter (37) sūrat l-ṣāfāt (Those Ranges in Ranks)

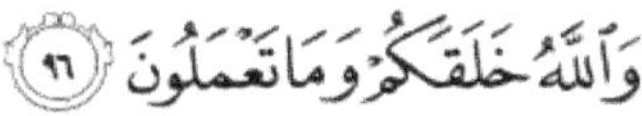

While Allah created you and that which you do?"

Sahih International Translation.

The Homecoming

Do you meet or see God at the end of the Journey? Even, when the Prophet(pbuh) went on his Night Journey and Ascension to Heaven, it is not clear whether he saw God.

Abdullah b. Shaqiq reported:

I said to Abu Dharr: Had I seen the Messenger of Allah, I would have asked him. He (Abu Dharr) said: What is that thing that you wanted to inquire of him? He said: I wanted to ask him whether he had seen his Lord. Abu Dharr said: I, in fact, inquired of him, and he replied: I saw Light.

Sahih Muslim 178b

Narrated 'Ikrimah:

that Ibn 'Abbas said (regarding the Ayah): The heart lied not in what he (ﷺ) saw (53:11). He said: "He saw Him with his heart."

Tirmidhi Vol. 5, Book 44, Hadith 3281

There are some interpretations of Authentic Hadith that claim that the Prophet(pbuh) did see Allah, but I am not getting into that debate.

Moses(pbuh) while trying to see God, fainted on the Mountain when the divine light appeared.

Maybe it is with your soul that you interact with God.

The Signs

So, how do you know that you succeeded in your journey? Are there any signs? Yes there are. Firstly, you should decrease in age during your journey if not physically, mentally for sure. You should return like a child. innocent and happy but overflowing with wisdom. Imagine a Child playing happily with pearls and eating butter and honey.

Jesus invited a little child to stand among them. "Truly I tell you," He said, "unless you change and become like little children, you will never enter the kingdom of heaven. Therefore, whoever humbles himself like this little child is the greatest in the kingdom of heaven. And whoever welcomes a little child like this in My name welcomes Me.

(Matthew 18:2-5) BSB

Secondly, the inner self or the soul which was turbulent before, should be calm and serene now.

A song of ascents, of David

My heart is not proud, O LORD,

my eyes are not haughty.

I do not aspire to great things

or matters too lofty for me.

Surely I have stilled and quieted my soul;

like a weaned child with his mother,

like a weaned child is my soul within me.

(Psalm 131) BRB

In the Quran, the Satisfied Soul is thus referred.

Chapter (89) sūrat l-fajr (The Dawn), verse 27-28

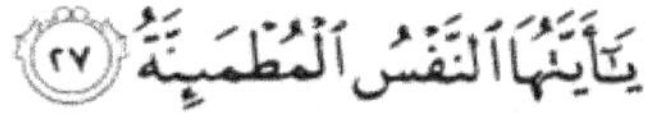

O soul that art at rest!

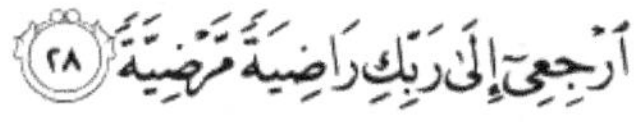

Return to your Lord, well-pleased (with him), well-pleasing (Him)

Translation of Shakir

The people of God who have made successful journeys are full of vigour and vitality, as if they were suddenly younger. That's because God has removed the burden of sin from their shoulders and souls, which was weighing them down.

Surah Ash-Sharh

أَلَمْ نَشْرَحْ لَكَ صَدْرَكَ ﴿١﴾

1. Did We not expand for you, [O Muhammad], your breast?

وَوَضَعْنَا عَنكَ وِزْرَكَ ﴿٢﴾

2. And We removed from you your burden

ٱلَّذِىٓ أَنقَضَ ظَهْرَكَ ﴿٣﴾

3. Which had weighed upon your back

Our Potential

Adam(pbuh) was fashioned by the Creator, and appointed as his Viceroy (Khalifa) on Earth. The moment the Ruh(spirit) was blown into the Body of Adam(pbuh), the Angles were commanded to prostate to him. Adam(pbuh) was given Knowledge by the All Wise, which was withheld from even the angles. These two facts, elevate him above the Angles. That's the station of Adam(pbuh) and being his progeny, we all have the potential, with the Grace of the Exalter of Ranks, to rise above the Angles.

The Rules Of The Court

Let's get back to where we were on the Highway, the vast majority of the people have taken the last exit. The seekers of The Most Gracious continue. The road ahead is full of barricades and this time, the Angles are checking everybody. What are they looking for, your religious credentials? Your book of good deeds? No! those were good till the last exit. They are checking if you know the code of proper conduct, for if you don't know how you should approach the Court of the King, you are not granted entry.

Adaab

The word in Arabic for character and manners is Akhlaq. The Urdu word Adaab means manners, but has overtime come to include character as well. I will be using the word Adaab from now on to talk about ethical conduct or how you should approach the Court of the Most Benevolent, or the Prophet or any True Servant.

Islam is not considered a new religion brought by Prophet Mohammed(pbuh) but rather as the religion of Abraham(pbuh). People asked the Prophet(pbuh) why has he come.

The Prophet Muhammad(pbuh) said "I was sent to perfect good character."

Malik, Book 47, Hadith 1643

At another instance,

The Prophet(pbuh) said 'The best among you are those who have the best manners and character '

(Bukhari, Vol 008, Book 073, Hadith Number 056B)

Prophet Muhammed(pbuh) had come, to teach you Adaab of this world and the Adaab of the court of the Most Merciful. The Adaab of this world teach you how to treat your parents, wife, children, friends and fellow human beings. His whole life he showed how character is built, that's the Sunnah of the Prophet.

The All Knowing commended the Prophet in the Quran-

Chapter (68) sūrat l-qalam (The Pen)

And verily, you (O Muhammad SAW) are on an exalted standard of character.

So, his whole mission was to uplift our character and manners. If you pray regularly and do all the other rituals and sacrifices and they don't improve your character and manners, forgive me for saying that you did not gain anything (and God Knows Best). You are missing the purpose. The prayer and the recitation of the Quran is supposed to soften your heart, if that is not happening, you are not doing it properly.

These days you see groups of people fighting and debating over the sunnah and each claiming to be better followers of the Sunnah. Don't you think they are missing the very objective?

Respect For The Prophet(Pbuh)

What's the Adaab for approaching the prophet? That you learn from the way Sahabas(companions of the Prophet) interacted with him, and there are abundant examples in the Hadith for you to learn from.

A famous Persian saying,

با خدا دیوانہ باش و با محمد ﷺ ہوشیار

You can go crazy (in love) in front of God but be careful when you are before Muhammed(pbuh).

What is meant is that the All Merciful might forgive you if you fall short in respect to Him, but He will not tolerate any disrespect shown to the Prophet(pbuh).

The Adaab of the Prophet(pbuh)

Let's talk about how Prophet Muhammed(pbuh) approached the All Mighty. He called himself a slave of the All Merciful and lowered himself and denied his own free will. His duty was to find the will of the Master and fulfil it. The All Merciful called His beloved Prophet by many beautiful names. He was not a slave in the eyes of the All Mighty that was just the Adaab of the Prophet and the All Mighty was pleased with his modesty. More the Prophet lowered himself, more exalted he was with the All Compassionate.

The Prophets(pbuh) always highlighted the fact, that he was unlettered, while he had the keys to the Treasures of Knowledge of God

Consider the case of a father with many children, in the beginning he loves them all equally. One of the sons, however, obeys whatever the father says, even if it goes against his wishes. Knowing his father well, he guesses beforehand the wishes of the father and fulfils them. He calls himself the slave of his father. What do you think the father will call him? He will out of love call him with many names, like my beloved son, the light of my eye, the comfort of my heart and so on.

I am not saying, we should not consider ourselves as slaves of the All Mighty. Following the sunnah and the Adaab of the Prophet is the fastest way to reach the Court of the King.

Adaab Of Other Prophets(pbut)

After tasting the forbidden fruit, whatever that stands for, Adam(pbuh) realized that He has gone against the wishes of his Benevolent Creator, guilt overtook him and he cried for a long time but did not know what to say. The King looked upon him in mercy and gave these words so that Adam(pbuh) and his Wife could approach Him.

Chapter (7) sūrat l-aʿrāf (The Heights), verse 23

قَالَا رَبَّنَا ظَلَمْنَا أَنفُسَنَا وَإِن لَّمْ تَغْفِرْ لَنَا وَتَرْحَمْنَا لَنَكُونَنَّ مِنَ ٱلْخَٰسِرِينَ ﴿٢٣﴾

"Our Lord, we have wronged ourselves, and if You do not forgive us and have mercy upon us, we will surely be among the losers"

Likewise, Jonah approached the King, from the belly of the fish.

Chapter (21) sūrat l-anbiyāa (The Prophets), verse 87

وَذَا ٱلنُّونِ إِذ ذَّهَبَ مُغَاضِبًا فَظَنَّ أَن لَّن نَّقْدِرَ عَلَيْهِ فَنَادَىٰ فِى ٱلظُّلُمَٰتِ أَن لَّآ إِلَٰهَ إِلَّآ أَنتَ سُبْحَٰنَكَ إِنِّى كُنتُ مِنَ ٱلظَّٰلِمِينَ ۝

And [mention] the man of the fish, when he went off in anger and thought that We would not decree [anything] upon him. And he called out within the darknesses, "There is no deity except You; exalted are You. Indeed, I have been of the wrongdoers."

Sahih International Translation.

Jesus(pbuh) washed the feet of his disciples. Is that a part of your regular religion? No, it's your training in Adaab, which isn't apart from religion.

Respect For All The Prophets

Now let's talk about the respect you should have for the Prophets(pbut) that came before Prophet Mohammed(pbuh). Examine what Allah commands us in this regard.

Chapter (2) sūrat l-baqarah (The Cow)

ءَامَنَ ٱلرَّسُولُ بِمَآ أُنزِلَ إِلَيْهِ مِن رَّبِّهِۦ وَٱلْمُؤْمِنُونَ ۚ كُلٌّ ءَامَنَ بِٱللَّهِ وَمَلَـٰٓئِكَتِهِۦ وَكُتُبِهِۦ وَرُسُلِهِۦ لَا نُفَرِّقُ بَيْنَ أَحَدٍ مِّن رُّسُلِهِۦ ۚ وَقَالُوا۟ سَمِعْنَا وَأَطَعْنَا ۖ غُفْرَانَكَ رَبَّنَا وَإِلَيْكَ ٱلْمَصِيرُ ﴿٢٨٥﴾

The Messenger has believed in what was revealed to him from his Lord, and [so have] the believers. All of them have believed in Allah and His angels and His books and His messengers, [saying], "We make no distinction between any of His messengers." And they say, "We hear and we obey. [We seek] Your forgiveness, our Lord, and to You is the [final] destination."

Translation of Sahih International.

Here we are told not to compare the Prophets (peace be upon them). The reason I am bringing this is because a few people in their ignorance, show respect to only Prophet Mohammed(pbuh) and compare other Prophets(pbut) to him and (God forbid) belittle them. May Allah forgive us.

Narrated Abu Huraira:

Two persons, a Muslim and a Jew, quarreled. The Muslim said, "By Him Who gave Muhammad superiority over all the people! The Jew said, "By Him Who gave Moses superiority over all the people!" At that the Muslim raised his hand and slapped the Jew on the face. The Jew went to the

Prophet and informed him of what had happened between him and the Muslim. The Prophet (ﷺ) sent for the Muslim and asked him about it. The Muslim informed him of the event. The Prophet (ﷺ) said, "Do not give me superiority over Moses, for on the Day of Resurrection all the people will fall unconscious and I will be one of them, but I will be the first to gain consciousness, and will see Moses standing and holding the side of the Throne (of Allah). I will not know whether (Moses) has also fallen unconscious and got up before me, or Allah has exempted him from that stroke."

Sahih Bukhari 2411

And

Narrated Abu Huraira:

The Prophet (ﷺ) said, "None should say that I am better than Yunus bin Matta."

Sahih Bukhari 3416

I think the reason Jonah(pbuh) is mentioned and I want to say this without implying any disrespect. Jonah(pbuh) being the only Prophet we know of in the Quran that Allah got angry at. I have already quoted the verse earlier for your reference.

Asma ul Husna (The Beautiful Names of Allah)

Do you think that the beautiful names of The All Mighty, came down only in Arabic, and only in the Quran? The Prophets and people that existed before, did not have possession of them.

Chapter (16) sūrat l-naḥl (The Bees), verse 36

وَلَقَدۡ بَعَثۡنَا فِى كُلِّ أُمَّةٍ رَّسُولًا أَنِ ٱعۡبُدُواْ ٱللَّهَ وَٱجۡتَنِبُواْ ٱلطَّٰغُوتَۖ فَمِنۡهُم مَّنۡ هَدَى ٱللَّهُ وَمِنۡهُم مَّنۡ حَقَّتۡ عَلَيۡهِ ٱلضَّلَٰلَةُۚ فَسِيرُواْ فِى ٱلۡأَرۡضِ فَٱنظُرُواْ كَيۡفَ كَانَ عَٰقِبَةُ ٱلۡمُكَذِّبِينَ ۝

And verily, We have sent among every Ummah (community, nation) a Messenger (proclaiming): "Worship Allah (Alone), and avoid (or keep away from) Taghut (all false deities, etc. i.e. do not worship Taghut besides Allah)."

Messengers were sent to all the people, obviously speaking different languages. They called upon Allah with the names provided to them in their language. Would you not consider the names used by the Great Prophets of the past like, Moses(pbuh), Esa(pbuh) and Abraham(pbuh), as beautiful.

Chapter (17) sūrat l-isrā (The Night Journey), verse 110

قُلِ ٱدْعُوا۟ ٱللَّهَ أَوِ ٱدْعُوا۟ ٱلرَّحْمَٰنَ ۖ أَيًّا مَّا تَدْعُوا۟ فَلَهُ ٱلْأَسْمَآءُ ٱلْحُسْنَىٰ ۚ وَلَا تَجْهَرْ بِصَلَاتِكَ وَلَا تُخَافِتْ بِهَا وَٱبْتَغِ بَيْنَ ذَٰلِكَ سَبِيلًا ﴿١١٠﴾

Say (O Muhammad SAW): "Invoke Allah or invoke the Most Beneficent (Allah), by whatever name you invoke Him (it is the same), for to Him belong the Best Names.

Is Allah, a name given for the first time in the Quran. No, the pagans of Mecca were familiar with, and called upon, that name, before the revelation of the Quran. If you had said Rahman (Most Beneficent), I would have agreed with you, for the people of Mecca, were comfortable with calling upon Allah but Rahman (Most Beneficent) was new to them.

So, before you correct someone saying Khuda Hafiz, and instruct him to say Allah Hafiz, know that they are both beautiful names of Allah. Don't put down one name over other just because at some point in history it was referred to or is still referred by some people of other faith to point to their God. For all beautiful names belong to Allah.

For God, is only One, and when you call upon a beautiful name, you only mean to call upon the One True God. It's all in your intention, for God knows who you are referring to even before you utter a beautiful name.

Tears of Love

A lot of people suggest that we should cry before the Lord, while praying. If tears do not come, they suggest that we should think of some tragic event in our lives and then the tears will come. That's just Drama. Please refrain from crying in congregation, unless overwhelmed by the Love of God. The tears come naturally when you truly love God, and you should hide them as pearls. Try to approach your Lord when in solitude, like the late-night prayer (Tahajjud), and no one's watching. Then if the tears come, let them come for the heart, is no longer yours to claim.

On A Leaving Note,

Please do not consider yourselves as pious or Holy, for that's the garb of Allah.

Anas ibn Malik reported:

The Prophet, peace and blessings be upon him, said, "All of the children of Adam are sinners, and the best sinners are those who repent."
Tirmidhī 2499

God Knows Best.

References

1. Bible Hub. https://biblehub.com/

2. Gazzâlî, (1994). İhya'u Ulumi'd-din (A. Aydın, Trans.). İstanbul, Turkey: Aydın Yayınları.

3. Gazzali, (2000). Kimyâ-yı Saadet (A. Arslan, Trans.). İstanbul, Turkey: Merve Yayınları.

4. Iqbal, Allama. Jawaab e Shikwa

5. Islamic-Awareness. https://www.islamic-awareness.org/quran/contrad/external/mary

6. Jilani, Abdul Qadir. Futuh Al-Ghaib

7. Jilani, Abdul Qadir. Purification of the Mind (Jila' Al-Khatir)

8. Khan, Mohsin. (Trans) Quranic Arabic Corpus. https://corpus.quran.com/

9. Makdisi, George. Aḥmad ibn Ḥanbal. Encyclopædia Britannica. https://www.britannica.com/biography/Ahmad-ibn-Hanbal

10. Shah, R. R. (2015). Saint Thomas Aquinas and Imam al-Ghazali on the attainment of happiness. The International Journal of Religion and Spirituality in Society, 6, 15–29.

11. Sunnah.com. https://sunnah.com

12. Yurdakök, İsmail. Court Minutes Of The Ahmad B. Hanbal